Copyright©

About the Author

Dr. Kim Cliett Long is a lifelong educator. She has worked at all levels of education from Pre-K to Higher Education. She enjoys traveling, reading, researching historical topics, sewing and watching historical documentaries.

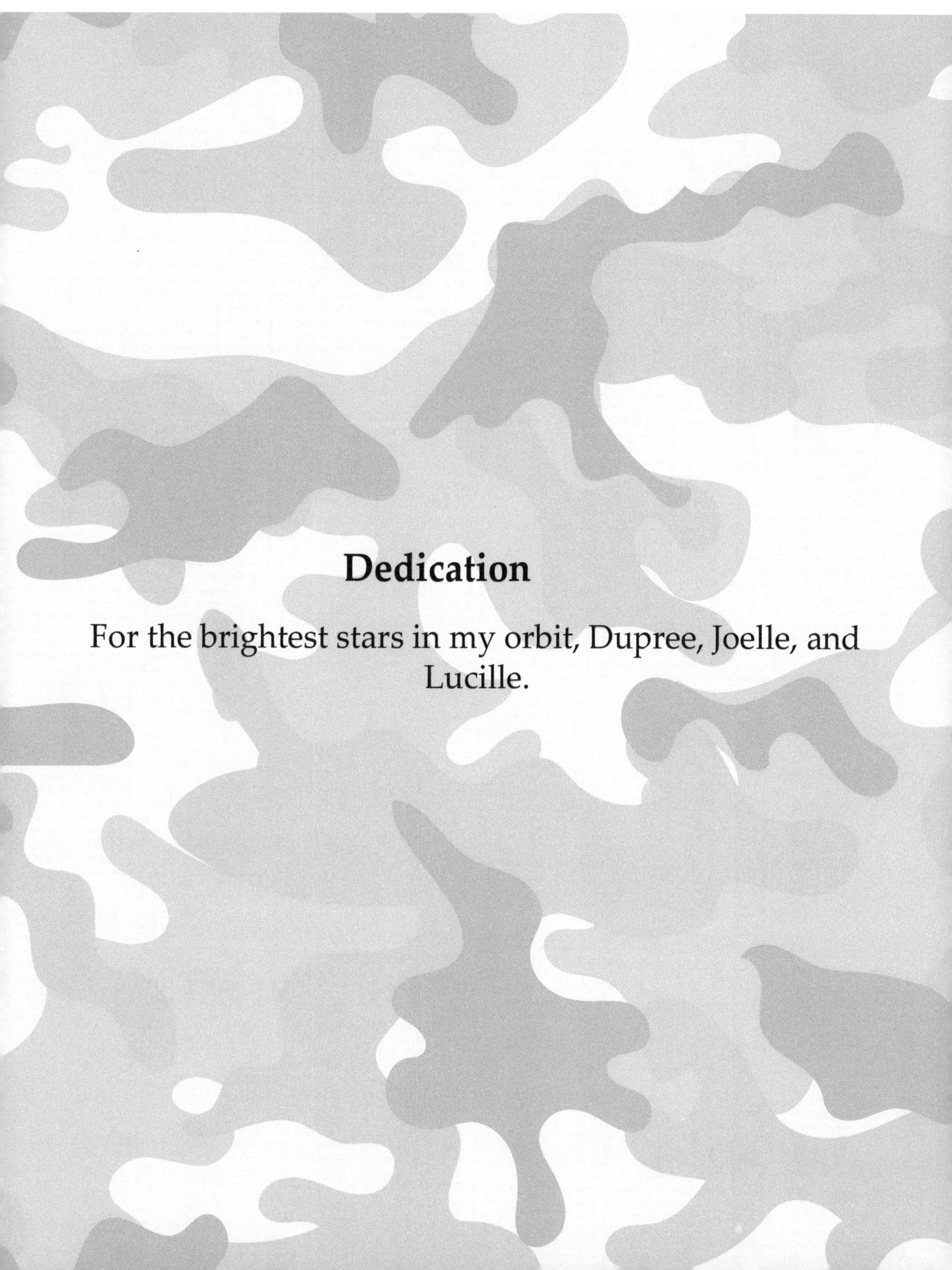
Dedication

For the brightest stars in my orbit, Dupree, Joelle, and
Lucille.

A
IS FOR..
Advancing forward towards the Enemy.

B
IS FOR..
Battle Positions that we
make for a sure victory.

C IS FOR..

Chaplain where all the prayers and sermons come from.

D IS FOR..

Deployment of the soldiers to know where they are located when troubles come.

E IS FOR..

Embarkation which brings soldiers
and cargo into the ships or planes.

F
IS FOR..
File the troops straight into solid lanes.

G
IS FOR..
Ground Zero where a horrible
weapon hit.

H IS FOR..
Head meaning the first person in front of a file or unit.

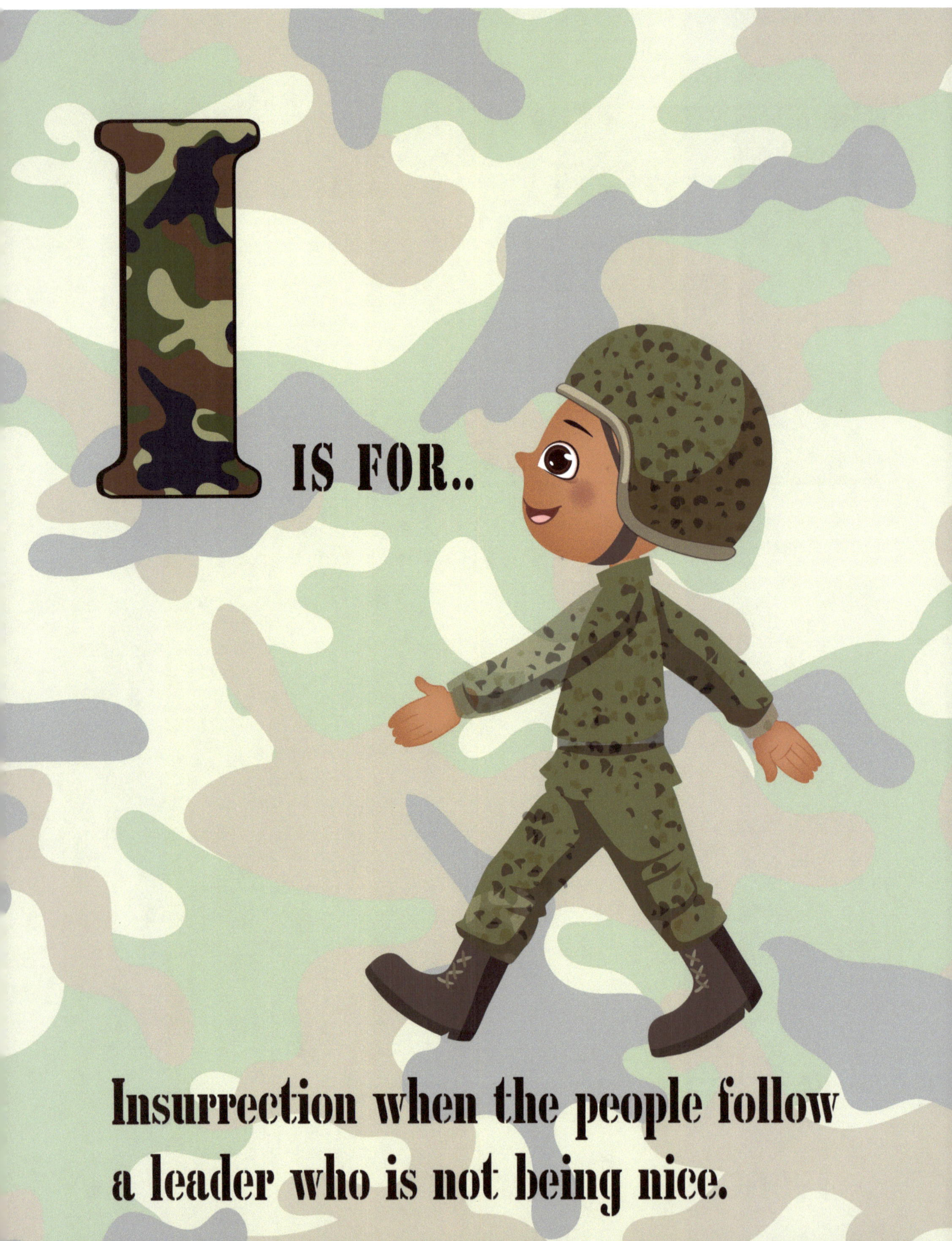

I
IS FOR..
Insurrection when the people follow
a leader who is not being nice.

Jamming or blocking the radio signals over mountains or fields of rice.

K IS FOR..
Key Terrain the place where the soldiers must patrol and drive the Rover.

Left and Right Flank at the edge of any group whenever they crossover.

M IS FOR.
Mission that talks about the task at hand.

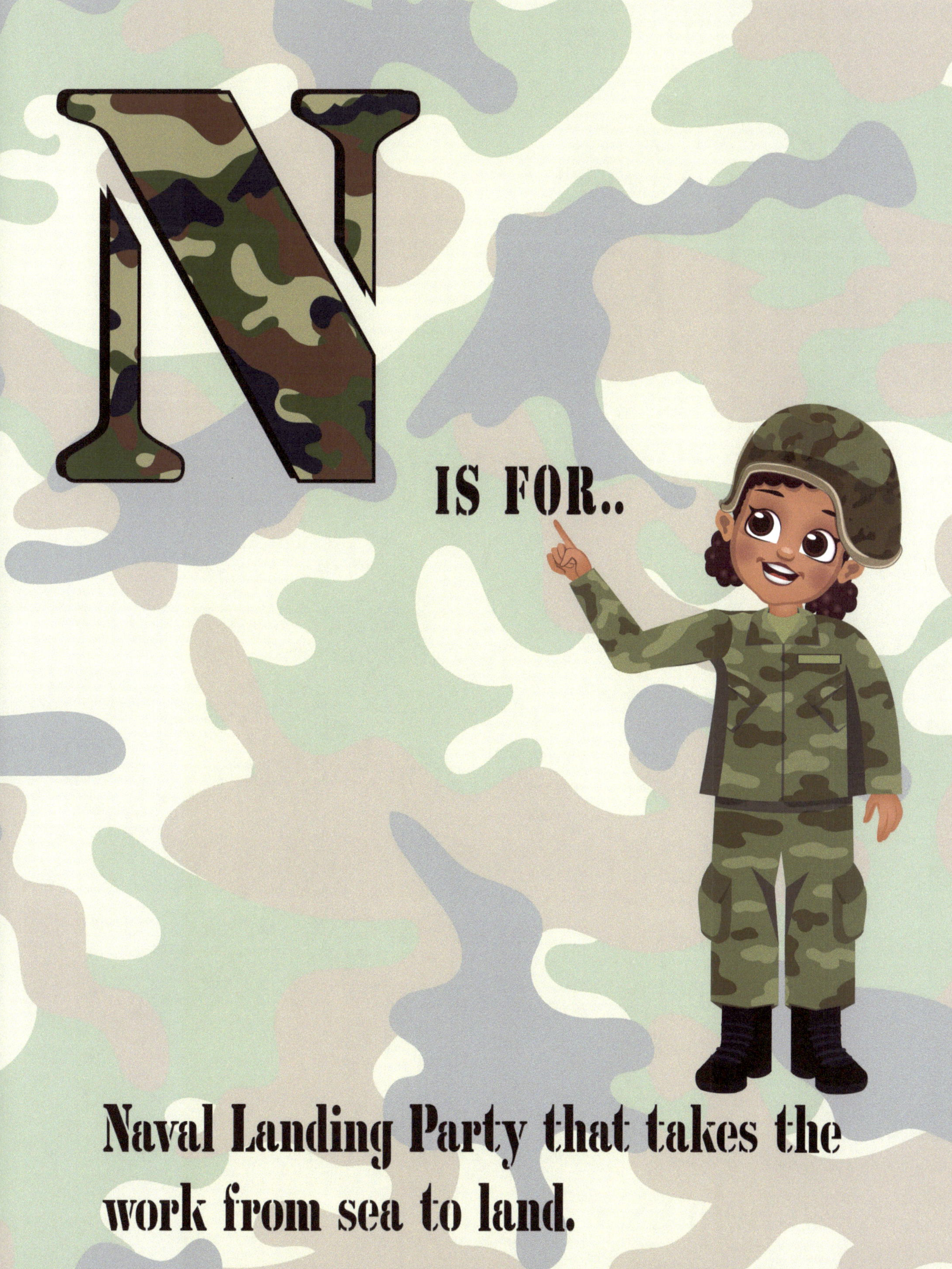

N IS FOR..
Naval Landing Party that takes the work from sea to land.

O IS FOR..

Organic essential forming of teams
to help us win.

P

IS FOR..

Patrol by a select group who
protect all to not face defeat.

Quick Time for the cadence of moving two steps for every second's beat.

R IS FOR..

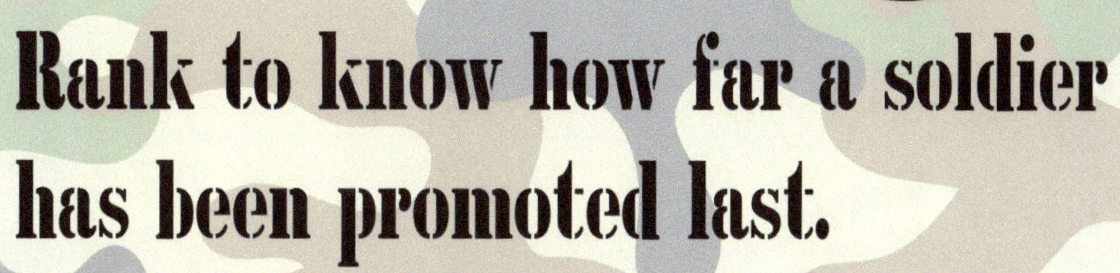

Rank to know how far a soldier has been promoted last.

S IS FOR..

Security to serve and protect the cause from spies or blasts.

T
IS FOR..
Terrain where all things happen on the ground from planning until the troop has an achievement.

U
IS FOR..
Underground where people move
and work in secret.

V

IS FOR..

Vetting to make sure all plans are executed exactly right.

Withdrawal as the team retreats
to bring a clearer plan to light.

 **IS FOR..**

eXplosive things that go boom and burn all around.

Yawing as the Captain steers the vehicle away horizontally before it is found.

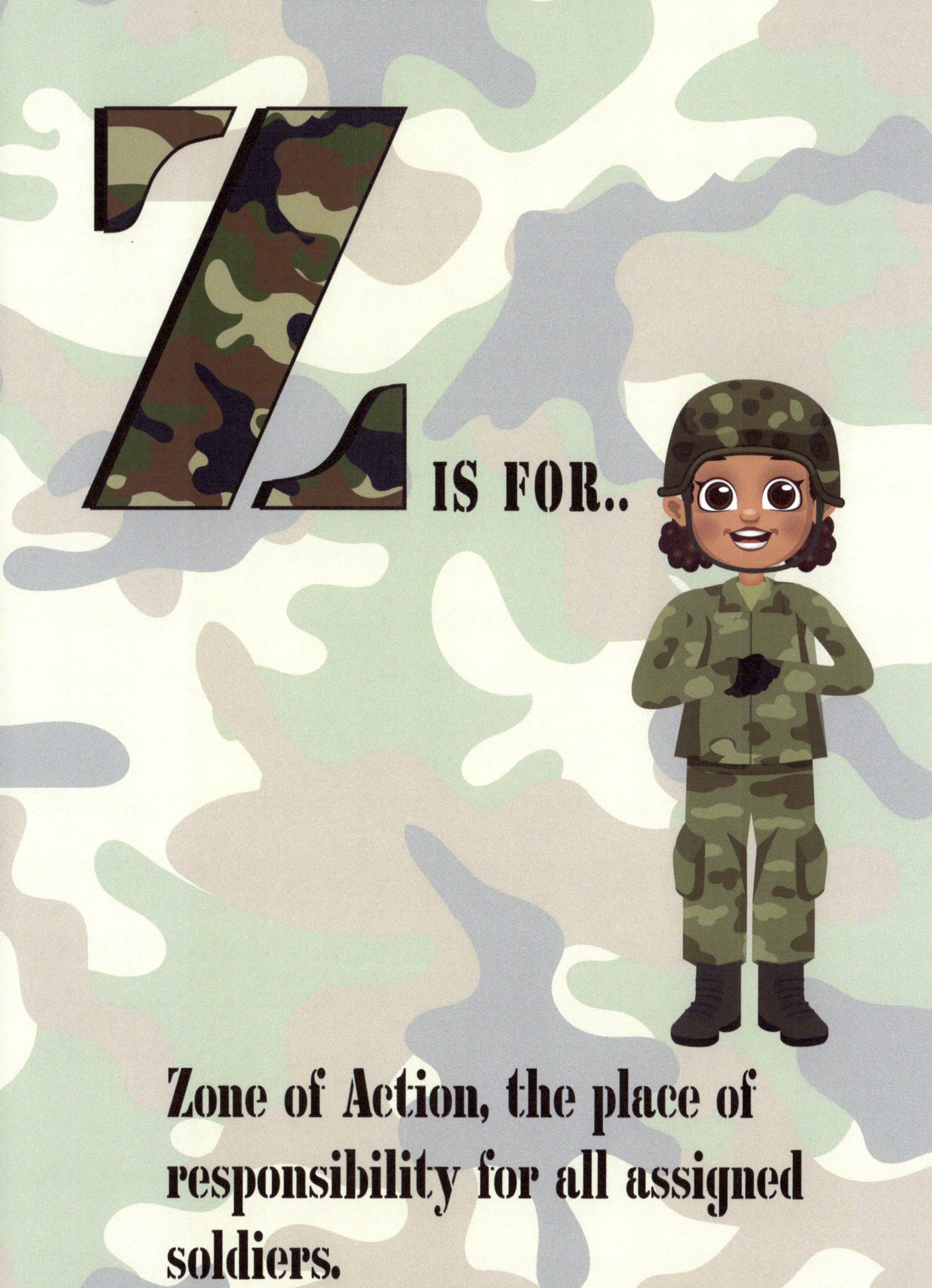

Z IS FOR..
Zone of Action, the place of responsibility for all assigned soldiers.